Jack the Ripper
A Life of Crime

Alexander Kennedy

Amazon.com/author/alexanderkennedy

Contents

Foreword

As awful as it sounds, we love serial killers. Or, perhaps, it is more accurate to say that we love to read about serial killers, but that doesn't quite cover it, does it? It's a well-documented fact that humanity has been fascinated with the dark and the macabre pretty much since the first story was written. The Epic of Gilgamesh is a story of violence—heroism and sacrifice, too, of course, but those are not the elements that made it last; it's the cruelty of the gods that make that story particularly enduring. The tradition of displaying such cruelty for all to see—and yes, to delight in—continued across generations, leading to such masters of horror as Edgar Allen Poe, Stephen King, and modern filmmakers like Wes Craven and the incomparable Alfred Hitchcock.

But the truth is that real crimes and humanity's true monsters hold a much greater thrall over people than any fiction. And, unfortunately, some of those monsters were, in fact, more monstrous than any fiction.

Jack the Ripper is, perhaps, the most notorious serial killer in history. He only claimed a handful of victims, which does not put him at the top of any list; his barbarism and violence was certainly villainous, but they were not, as such things are measured, much worse than most—he did, at least, kill his victims before he performed his mutilations. Nor was he the only serial killer who escaped capture: the Atlanta Ripper (whose nickname was a legacy of Jack's), the Texarkana Phantom, the New Orleans Axeman, and, of course, the Zodiac Killer are just some of the notorious murderers who were never found.

4

Yet most people have never heard of more than one of the above, while everybody has heard of Jack the Ripper. His story has been told countless times across countless formats, from poems and stories to movies and plays, and people simply cannot get enough.

Why, then, are we so interested in the murderer of five prostitutes in Victorian London? That, along with many of the other mysteries surrounding the phantom named Jack the Ripper, is what this book seeks to unravel.

The truth, as you'll find out, is definitely stranger than fiction.

Introduction

Jack the Ripper was "born," so to speak, in the early morning hours of Friday, August 31, 1888, when a cart driver named Charles Lechmere happened across the grotesquely mutilated body of Mary Ann Nichols in London's impoverished Whitechapel district.

The 43-year-old prostitute had just become the first victim of the notorious serial killer who has horrified and fascinated generations of people from the Victorian era right up until today. Astonishingly, the man later identified as the murderer was Lewis Carroll, the well-known author of Alice's Adventures in Wonderland and numerous other books.

Or something like that.

Actually, Carroll was just one of the more than 100 people whose names have been bandied about over the years in the search for Jack the Ripper. In that time, countless detectives, criminologists, pioneering profilers, novelists, psychologists, and others have put their minds to the task of sifting through the evidence and identifying the elusive killer once and for all.

Some of the "suspects" various researchers have identified over the years may well have been the likely killer. Others—Lewis Carroll among them—are the longest of long shots. Carroll, the pen name of scholar Charles Dodgson, only came under suspicion in 1996, more than 100 years after the crime spree.

In Jack the Ripper: Light-Hearted Friend, author Richard Wallace built his case against Carroll entirely upon "secret messages" confessing to the crimes that he claimed to have found in Carroll's extensive writings. While many experts quickly denounced the theory as a flight of fancy, Wallace's claims did get a lot of attention when the book was excerpted in Harper's Magazine.

Still, nearly 130 years after the grisly crimes, what is known about Jack the Ripper's true identity comes down to this: if he wasn't a famous children's author, he was a mentally ill Polish immigrant, or a Whitechapel bootmaker—or a suicidal barrister, a medical student, a poet or a prince. Or even a female midwife one investigator dubbed "Jill the Ripper," a theory advanced by Sir Arthur Conan Doyle, Sherlock Holmes's creator, who was himself suspected by others.

Or someone else.

And we know this—the first serial murderer who ever completely captured the world's attention during his (or her) gruesome crime spree still has a hold on our imaginations. Jack the Ripper's identity remains unknown, but together, the records he and his pursuers left behind, the lives of his victims, and the investigations of later experts paint a powerful picture of the darkness in his soul.

Part 1:
Terror in the East End

"My knife's so nice and sharp I want to get to work right away if I get a chance."—Jack the Ripper

Chapter 1:
Jack the Ripper Goes to Work

"They say I'm a doctor now. ha ha."—**Jack the Ripper**

Jack the Ripper's true identity is not the only still-unsolved mystery associated with the quick crime spree that horrified and fascinated millions of people around the world in the summer and fall of 1888. To this day, amateur and professional "Ripperologists" disagree on not only who was responsible, but on how many women he murdered, and who they were.

Even the name we know him by is a mystery of its own. If, as most authorities believe, his first victim was Mary Ann Nichols, killed on August 31, it was nearly a month before the police and public began calling him Jack the Ripper.

That was the signature on a chilling letter the murderer—or someone claiming to be—sent to the Central News Agency in London. The letter was addressed to "Dear Boss" and written in red ink (because, the writer taunted, "the proper red stuff... went thick like glue and I cant [sic] use it"). Initially, it was dismissed as a hoax when it arrived on September 27, and it sat at the news agency for two days before anyone thought to turn it over to the police.

Like the press, the police were at first skeptical about the authenticity of the letter, which included a threat: "I love my work and I want to start again." But they had no choice other than to take the threat seriously the next day when the serial killer claimed two more victims in the span of just an hour or so. Desperate for leads and under intense pressure to make an arrest, the police released the letter the next day, and the public and press both seized on the grim moniker from that day on.

Still, there was reason to doubt, then and now, that the letter actually came from the murderer (who until the message went public had been known variously as the Whitechapel Murderer, the Red Fiend, or, based on a dead-end lead, as Leather Apron). A journalist named George Sims, for one, dismissed "Jack the Ripper" as "a gruesome wag, a grim practical joker," and insisted that "the whole business is a farce." Sims was also one of many who suspected that the letter had been written by a journalist intent on further stirring an already roiling pot to drive up circulation even higher than the unprecedented levels it had reached thanks to the Ripper. (One paper, The Star, saw its circulation hit 232,000 buyers a day, for example).

Like Sims, however, a number of officials continued to have doubts. Sir Charles Warren, Commissioner of Police of the Metropolis, wrote to the British Home Office that, "...I think the whole thing a hoax but of course we are bound to try & ascertain the writer in any case."

And more than twenty years after the crimes, Robert Anderson, who had been head of the detective department on the case, wrote in his memoirs, "I will only add here that the 'Jack the Ripper' letter which is preserved in the Police Museum at New Scotland Yard is the creation of an enterprising London Journalist."

Jack the Ripper: Case Closed, a 2009 book by historian Andrew Cook, took that argument even further. Cook claimed that the murders, which he conceded were real, were not committed by a single person, but were unrelated. Both the "Dear Boss" letter and the whole notion of a serial killer were the fabrications of reporters, Cook concluded.

Real or not, that letter—and the countless ones that followed, some of them at least somewhat credible, but most of them easily discounted—played a large role in turning the case into a worldwide sensation.

The Whitechapel Murders File

The crimes were gruesome, the newspapers of the day were hungry for sensational stories, modern scientific criminology and profiling were in their infancy, and Whitechapel was an impoverished, crime-ridden, immigrant neighborhood right out of a Charles Dickens novel. It was an area where many of the social and economic issues of thc day could be seen in a bright light, and both the contempt some people felt for its residents and the compassion others felt only served to heighten public interest in the case.

By most accounts, the brief and bloody career of Jack the Ripper resulted in the deaths of five women, all prostitutes in London's East End, the first killed on August 31, the last on November 9, 1888. That, at least, is the consensus of both contemporary investigators and later researchers, who settled on what they call the five "canonical murders." Those were connected by not only time and location, but—more importantly—by modus operandi, the distinctive and barbarous way in which the women were murdered and then mutilated.

In all, the Whitechapel Murder File for the period includes eleven cases that have at times been considered possible Ripper crimes by some writers. Others have moved in the other direction, attributing only four of the canonical murders to Jack the Ripper. But the clear and unique similarities in the ways that Mary Ann Nichols (August 31), Annie Chapman (September 8), Elizabeth Stride (September 30), Catherine Eddowes (September 30), and Mary Kelly (November 9) were murdered convinced hundreds of investigators that the killings were the work of one man.

The Ripper's Modus Operandi Becomes Clear

The murders were brutal, and the subsequent mutilation was ghastly. By piecing together the evidence conveyed by the bodies themselves, police and medical professionals concluded that the women were strangled first. Then the Ripper went to work with his knife, slashing their throats from left to right before ripping open their abdomens and disemboweling most of the victims in a progressively gruesome manner.

Some he mutilated by removing the uterus and a kidney, or part of one. By the time he assaulted Mary Kelly, the last victim in the canon, however, his butchery knew no bounds. Thomas Bond, the physician who performed the post mortem examination on Kelly, detailed its extent in his report.

"The body was lying naked in the middle of the bed, the shoulders flat, but the axis of the body inclined to the left side of the bed. The head was turned on the left cheek. The left arm was close to the body with the forearm flexed at a right angle & lying across the abdomen. The right arm was slightly abducted from the body & rested on the mattress, the elbow bent & the forearm supine with the fingers clenched.

"The legs were wide apart, the left thigh at right angles to the trunk & the right forming an obtuse angle with the pubes. The whole of the surface of the abdomen & thighs was removed & the abdominal cavity emptied of its viscera. The breasts were cut off, the arms mutilated by several jagged wounds & the face hacked beyond recognition of the features. The tissues of the neck were severed all round down to the bone," Bond wrote.

"The viscera were found in various parts viz: the uterus & Kidneys with one breast under the head, the other breast by the Rt foot, the Liver between the feet, the intestines by the right side & the spleen by the left side of the body. The flaps removed from the abdomen and thighs were on a table. The bed clothing at the right corner was saturated with blood, & on the floor beneath was a pool of blood covering about 2 feet square...The face was gashed in all directions the nose cheeks, eyebrows and ears being partly removed. The lips were blanched & cut by several incisions running obliquely down to the chin. There were also numerous cuts extending irregularly across all the features."

The disfigurement of Kelly was so extreme that her lover had difficulty confirming her identity, and the medical examiners were never able to confirm that she had had her throat slit from left to right, like the other victims.

At the other extreme, the body of Elizabeth Stride was relatively untouched, although her throat was slashed in the characteristic left to right manner. But that fact coupled with the nearby murder of Catherine Eddowes less than an hour later led police to conclude that the attack on Stride had been interrupted. If so, as is likely, Jack the Ripper made up for it when he encountered Eddowes, whose uterus and left kidney he took with him when he escaped, and whose face he slashed along with her throat.

Jack the Ripper's penchant for such macabre surgeries led many to speculate that he had medical training and, not surprisingly, the long list of suspects has included medical students and physicians. London's medical community in 1888, however, was quick to denounce the speculation, insisting that the Ripper's technique was crude and there was no evidence he had any advanced knowledge of anatomy.

The Fascination with Jack Never Ends

There is yet another mystery that can be added to the list of unanswered, or unanswerable, questions about the case of Jack the Ripper: Why did it become one of the most famous crimes in history, one that not only caused a sensation at the time it was plastered across the daily papers, but one that has endured for nearly 130 years and shows no sign of fading from our collective imagination?

Hundreds of books have been written on the case, fiction and nonfiction, scholarly and fanciful. Sir Arthur Conan Doyle pinned it on a midwife, while modern crime writer Patricia Cornwell identified British painter William Sickert as the perpetrator. Hollywood films, documentaries, television programs, and web sites continue to spread, as do Jack the Ripper societies and Ripper-based Whitechapel tours.

But Jack the Ripper was not the first serial killer—that distinction is lost somewhere deep in history, because such people have always walked amongst us. Neither was he the "worst." Many others have killed far more victims, but few of them can rival him when it comes to holding our attention.

Some of the possible reasons for Jack's continued cultural influence have been discussed—the emerging power of the press in 1888, the nature of the crimes, the sociological dramas they highlighted—but the most significant reason for the enduring fascination may be the simplest and most obvious one: he got away with it, and society is unwilling to let a good mystery go.

Somewhere there are answers to who did it, how, and why. Human nature dictates that clues be examined and reexamined until those answers come to light.

Chapter 2:
The Investigation and the Birth of Profiling

"The Queen fears that the detective department is not as efficient as it might be."—**Queen Victoria**

The frustrated police decided to take a shot in the dark, and placed some scant "forlorn hope" in a new technique to help find a few clues. The investigators turned to "expert photographers with the latest type cameras" to get a glimpse of Jack the Ripper—through the eyes of his final victim.

The idea was to take photographs of Mary Kelly's lifeless eyes in the hope that the image of the last thing she saw—her killer—might still be visible on her retinas. If that sounds farfetched today, it wasn't that at all in the late-nineteenth and early-twentieth centuries.

The pseudoscience of optography was first mentioned over 200 years earlier when a Jesuit friar was said to have observed an image in the eye of a dissected frog. In the 1870s, optography became the subject of serious experimentation by Victorian Era scientists, and its potential applications in murder investigations were widely noted.

Boiled down, the theory was that, the eye being like a camera, it might be possible to "fix" an image left on the retina in the same way photographic chemicals capture an image on light-sensitive paper or metal plates. For several decades, the idea continued to interest researchers (optography experiments were carried out as recently as the 1970s) and the idea of a death image was a popular plot line in novels at the turn of the twentieth century.

Against that backdrop, it's not surprising that police employed the technique in the search for Jack the Ripper, as documented by Inspector Walter Dew. Like so much about the case, there are conflicting views about whether or not optography was in fact used in the Ripper case, but Dew's account has been accepted by most. Nevertheless, although multiple photographers took pictures of Mary Kelly's eyes using state-of-the-art cameras, "the result was negative," Dew wrote.

Policing Enters the Modern Age

Interestingly, police procedures in 1888 did not generally include using photography for what would now be considered a more conventional purpose—taking crime scene photos. Mary Kelly was photographed at the scene of her death, and pictures of some of the other victims were taken in the morgue, but there was no effort made to record visual evidence at the crime scenes, as later became standard procedure.

In fact, the Ripper's killing spree in many regards occurred on or just before the dawn of modern crime-solving practices, which is certainly one reason the crimes went unsolved. Not only was crime scene photography disregarded, but fingerprinting was still several years off, and the first forensic crime lab didn't open for another 22 years in Lyons, France.

And yet another now-familiar investigative technique—criminal profiling—only came about in the course of the search for Jack the Ripper. Dr. Thomas Bond, a police surgeon, was called in to the investigation specifically to provide a medical opinion on the killer's knowledge of anatomy. The question was highly significant, because the murderer's modus operandi, which included harvesting bodily organs, led many to believe that he had a medical background. Both medical students and practicing physicians came under suspicion, along with butchers and "horse slaughterers."

Bond examined the inquest records from the first four canonical murders (Nichols, Chapman, Stride, and Eddowes), and then performed the autopsy on Kelly himself. (It was just the day before Dr. Bond turned in his report that Kelly, victim number five, was killed.)

He concluded that all of the women had been killed by the same person and that the murderer did not have any medical knowledge, as some supposed.

"In each case the mutilation was inflicted by a person who had no scientific nor anatomical knowledge. In my opinion he does not even possess the technical knowledge of a butcher or horse slaughterer or any person accustomed to cut up dead animals," Bond wrote.

That was the crux of the question he had been asked, but Bond's detailed report went further. He provided many of the assumptions and conclusions that have guided researchers ever since. The report also includes the doctor's ruminations on the murderer's possible personality traits and lifestyle. This has been viewed by many as the first formal criminal profile, though it was not quite intended as such, and was primitive compared to modern standards.

Bond's analysis indicated that none of the women had struggled with their attacker and that all had been strangled before the knife was used. Four out of five had their throats cut from left to right, the fifth being too disfigured to make a determination, and four out of five were attacked from their right sides.

He also speculated about the weapon used after the women were strangled, estimating that it was "a strong knife at least six inches long, very sharp, pointed at the top and about an inch in width . . . no doubt a straight knife." Taken together, these and other observations in the report gave police and subsequent investigators a vivid picture of the crime scenes, and an understanding of how the murders may have been committed.

At the same time, it answered a question that nagged at the police on the case. They knew it was likely that the Ripper had passed by numerous potential witnesses, including some officers, while leaving the scenes of the quickly-discovered killings, presumably covered in blood after his butchery. Clearly, bloody hands and clothes should have given him away, yet nobody had noticed such a person.

Dr. Bond offered a medical explanation for that. Because the women were strangled first, slashing their throats would not produce the large amount of gushing blood that would normally be expected when the carotid arteries were cut. Therefore, "the murderer would not necessarily be splashed or deluged with blood, but his hands' and arms must have been covered and parts of his clothing must certainly have been smeared with blood."

A bulky overcoat, for one possibility, could have hidden the evidence.

The Birth of Criminal Profiling

Bond's major innovation, however, was not so much in his evaluation of the physical evidence as in the less tangible conclusions he drew. He ended his report with speculation about Jack the Ripper that he hoped would help police make an arrest. The murders were clearly committed by a very strong man, he surmised, and someone "of great coolness and daring."

"He must in my opinion be a man subject to periodical attacks of homicidal and erotic mania," Bond said. He went on to speculate that the murderer "may be in a condition sexually, that may be called satyriasis," the male equivalent of the more familiar term, nymphomania. "Religious mania" or a "revengeful or brooding condition of the mind" were other possible causes of the Ripper's homicidal rage, as Bond saw it, but he thought both explanations unlikely.

What was likely, he asserted, was that the man terrorizing Whitechapel was quiet, inoffensive, middle-aged, and probably a somewhat eccentric loner. Bond also offered a ray of hope to the harried police who remained under great pressure to solve the case. He guessed that the killer might be "living among respectable persons who have some knowledge of his character and habits and who may have grounds for suspicion that he is not quite right in his mind at times."

He suggested that the promise of a reward might help those respectable persons remember to do their civic duty.

It was a suggestion others had made and officials had resisted, and it came from Dr. Bond late in the game. He filed his report on November 10, the day after he performed the post mortem examination on the body of Mary Kelly. That November 9 murder in Whitechapel marked the end of Jack the Ripper's career.

One hundred years later, another profiler, this one with the benefit of sophisticated research and extensive experience, turned his attention to the Ripper case. John E. Douglas, Supervisory Special Agent at the FBI National Center for the Analysis of Violent Crime and Program Manager of Criminal Investigative Analysis, examined the case through the lenses of now commonly applied aspects as victimology, medical reports, and crime scene analysis, before arriving at a detailed profile in his 1988 report.

Douglas's findings were not all that different from Dr. Bond's in some regards. The killer, Douglas concluded, was an unmarried white male, probably between 28 and 36 years old, ordinary looking, socially detached, and with a "diminished emotional response toward his fellow man." His crimes were what would now be called "lust murders," characterized not by sexual assault—Jack the Ripper's victims were not raped—but by genital mutilation.

Rather than being notable for what Bond had called satyriasis, however, the FBI profiler concluded that Jack the Ripper was probably a person who had been raised by a passive or absent father and a domineering mother who likely was promiscuous and a heavy drinker—much like his prostitute victims.

In his eight-page report, Douglas also surmised that Jack the Ripper was a local who lived or worked in Whitechapel, drank in local pubs, and didn't stand out in any way in his daily life. He may have worked alone in a job such as a butcher or a mortician's assistant, "where he could vicariously experience his destructive fantasies." Significantly, Douglas also concluded that he had been interviewed, perhaps several times, by the police in the course of the investigation.

Common wisdom of the day, however, suggested that Jack the Ripper would be "odd or ghoulish in appearance," Douglas noted, and that belief led the investigators astray.

The Search for "Leather Apron"

Police in 1888 London may have lacked advanced forensics knowledge and techniques, but they did have one thing going for them: lots and lots of manpower. In the course of the investigation, they questioned more than two thousand people and further investigated at least three hundred of them, including seventy-six butchers and their employees, and they eventually took eighty people into custody, if only briefly. Because of the grisly postmortem slashings that marked the crimes, they paid particular attention to butchers, slaughterers, physicians, and others who wielded knives in their work.

One of them was John (or Jack) Pizer, also known as "Leather Apron" in the neighborhood and shortly in the press.

Leather Apron was the name area prostitutes knew him by as well, and that was the only name they had to share with police in the days after the first canonical murder. The women suspected him because he had already established himself as a menace, and as many as fifty of them told investigators so. They insisted that the man frequently extorted money from Whitechapel prostitutes, and beat those who wouldn't or couldn't pay. The street name they knew him by came from his habit of wearing a leather apron—a common garment for some tradesmen—at all times, they said.

That would have been a slight clue to pursue, but one officer, Sergeant William Thick, was able to identify Leather Apron as an unemployed Whitechapel slipper maker whose actual name was John Pizer, someone the officer had known for many years. The police hoped to search for Pizer quietly, but the London press went public with the suspicion before they could act.

On September 4, just four days after the Nichols murder and four days before the Chapman slaying, the papers broke the news of a possible suspect beneath sensational headlines proclaiming Leather Apron "The Only Name Linked with the Whitechapel Murders." (At that point, the Nichols murder was not yet seen as the first work of a new serial killer, but one of the several unsolved Whitechapel crimes).

When the news broke, Pizer, a Jewish immigrant from Poland, decided to lay low, as much for fear of attack by an angry mob as fear of the law. He had good reason to be afraid. Not only were many people outraged by the horrific crimes and frantic to catch the killer, but the specter of a murderous Leather Apron and the deliberately inflammatory news articles also tapped into a strong vein of anti-Semitism in 1888 London.

The Newspapers Fan the Flames

Whitechapel was a poor, largely immigrant neighborhood, and anti-immigrant Londoners found it a convenient target for their resentment. Days before Pizer was identified, the Star newspaper, for one, described the man police were seeking, as having a "sinister" expression, featuring small, glittering eyes and an "excessively repellent" grin.

"His name nobody knows, but they are all united in the belief that he is a Jew or of Jewish parentage, his face being of a marked Hebrew type," the paper reported.

The anti-Semitic outbursts that followed included intimidation, brawls, farfetched rumors of secret and bloody Jewish rituals, and bigotry from members of the police and public, who believed that "no Englishman could have perpetrated such a horrible crime." But it did nothing to catch the killer, who was just beginning his spree.

Sergeant Thick—who may have had it in for Pizer for personal reasons, by some accounts—took the slipper maker into custody on September 10. The arrest proved to be just one false step among what would be many. Pizer insisted he had no idea he was known in the district as Leather Apron, and denied even wearing one except to and from his former job. He also provided alibis for the time of both the August 31 and September 8 murders, including an exceptionally good one for the night of the Nichols killing. In the early hours of that morning, Pizer was staying at a lodging house in another part of the city, as a policeman he had spoken with about a fire on the docks later confirmed.

His rapid release, though, did little or nothing to erase the picture the newspapers had already painted. In the popular mind, and in the minds of the investigators, Jack the Ripper remained a "mysterious foreigner of dark complexion." As FBI profiler John Douglas suggested a century later, that image may have thrown the investigation off-track, causing officials to search for someone who was noticeably sinister, rather than the shy, unobtrusive man the killer likely was.

The Police Feel the Pressure

By mid-September, the public was growing impatient, the police were growing frustrated, and the press was ramping up its increasingly sensational coverage. And, despite a concerted investigation that massed the combined resources of multiple police departments, Scotland Yard, the British Home Office, and citizen groups, Jack the Ripper remained unidentified and still at large.

Not surprisingly, that brought down intense pressure on the police from every quarter.

Even Queen Victoria got involved. On October 1, the same day the "Dear Boss" letter first appeared in the Daily News, the queen "expressed her shock" about the murders in a telephone call she place to the Home Office. (She was an early adopter of the telephone, having been given a demonstration in 1878 by Alexander Graham Bell himself).

The following month, she put her concerns in writing in a November 13 letter to the Home Secretary. The polite but critical letter was later included in Christopher Hibbert's Queen Victoria in Her Letters and Journals.

"The Queen fears that the detective department is not so efficient as it might be. No doubt the recent murders in Whitechapel were committed in circumstances which made detection very difficult; still, the Queen thinks that, in the small area where these horrible crimes have been perpetrated, a great number of detectives might be employed, and that every possible suggestion might be carefully examined and, if practicable, followed. Have the cattle boats and passenger boats been examined? Has any investigation been made as to the number of single men occupying rooms by themselves? The murderer's clothes must be saturated with blood and must be kept somewhere. Is there sufficient surveillance at night? These are some of the questions that occur to the Queen on reading the account of this horrible crime."

Like so many armchair quarterbacks before and since, the Queen didn't really have any new thoughts to offer, but her interest in the case could only have increased the pressure on the police. In part, their efforts may have been hampered by bureaucratic glitches as much as the limitations of 1880s criminal science.

Early in the course of the Whitechapel Murders, the Metropolitan Police (Whitechapel Division) Criminal Investigation Department (CID), under the direction of Detective Inspector Edmund Reid, was responsible for investigating the murders. Scotland Yard joined in after the murder of Mary Ann Nichols, and the City of London Police after the Eddowes murder, which occurred just over the city line, in their jurisdiction.

Add to that an ad hoc citizens' patrol known as the Whitechapel Vigilance Committee, and there was no shortage of manpower, and no shortage of suspects, however farfetched or grounded in prejudice rather than evidence they might have been. At times, mobs formed and joined in police chases of people who were not even related to the case, but whom the crowds immediately assumed might be Jack the Ripper.

The fact that the CID, at the center of the investigation, was led by a new director after years of turmoil among the leadership and sinking morale among the rank and file didn't help either. Neither did the fact that Robert Anderson, the new CID head, was out of the country for a critical month spanning the Ripper's second, third, and fourth murders. In Anderson's absence—a rest in Switzerland to recover from the longstanding stresses at the CID—Sir Charles Warren, the Metropolitan Police Commissioner, appointed Chief Inspector Donald Swanson to run the show.

As might be expected, the Victorian-era press didn't pull any punches in their criticisms, and sometimes mockery, of the police. Often, they were portrayed as bumblers, very much like those who would come into popular culture a few decades later in the form of Mack Sennett's "Keystone Kops" silent films.

At other times, the press attacks were harsher, and they ultimately played a role in further turmoil in the law enforcement leadership. On November 9, the same day that Jack the Ripper claimed his fifth and final victim, Sir Charles Warren submitted his resignation after a barrage of criticism.

To some extent, Warren's resignation came about as a result of the bad press, but some researchers point to something deeper as well. The unsuccessful Ripper investigation, they said, also presented an opportunity for Warren's political enemies to exploit the situation and undermine a powerful figure with whom they had previously clashed and lost.

The supposed incompetence of the police was the subject of Blind Man's Buff, a stinging cartoon by John Tenniel that appeared in the September 22, 1888 issue of the satirical magazine, Punch.

Chapter 3:
"The Whole of the East End Is Starving"

"One fine day the people about here will go desperate."—
Margaret Harkness

It was not only the anti-immigrant and anti-Jewish sentiments that had been simmering for several years that Jack the Ripper brought into sharp focus. The case also became a focal point for already sharp divisions between social and economic factions in England's rigid, class-conscious society, and between the staunch traditionalists and the crusading reformers and socialists who made up the country's upper crust and intelligentsia.

That landscape provided the background against which the victims, the killer and the killings, the investigation, and the public response can be understood.

The Upper Crust and the Social Reformers

One side saw the Whitechapel Murders and the crime-ridden neighborhood they brought to public attention as emblematic of the danger of England being overrun by foreigners. That narrative played into the hands of a segment of the upper class, as well as many government officials and journalists.

Some of the police investigating the crimes and much of the press also shared in that view. The anti-Semitism the crimes stirred up provided cover for the police to target Jewish socialists, with at least tacit support from higher-ups who saw an opportunity to push back hard against political opponents on the left. It was only when public anger directed at Whitechapel's Jewish community became so intense that officials feared riots that police backtracked to cool tempers down. The concern was so great by that point that hundreds of policemen were deployed to the East End after Annie Chapman's murder to keep order and prevent a full-scale pogrom.

On the other side, the Ripper case drew massive attention to conditions in London's teeming slums. Some reporters who went into the area to cover the crimes also ended up writing about the horrid conditions they found there. The case gave a new urgency to the reforms some philanthropists and social critics already felt were needed.

The murders, they said, were evidence of a "crisis of conscience" in British society, and reformers went to work drawing up plans for improved conditions in the rough and tumble neighborhood. Better housing, better street lighting, new job opportunities (in laundries) for women driven into prostitution by extreme poverty, and more "Bible women" were some the ideas considered. One letter writer to The Times asserted that the crimes "would not be in vain... if public conscience awakes to consider the life which these horrors reveal."

The great playwright and social critic George Bernard Shaw went even further. Shaw suggested in one letter that Jack the Ripper was actually a social reformer himself, committing his gruesome crimes specifically to bring public attention to inhuman living conditions.

Of course, that wasn't a serious claim, and Shaw was well known for using often biting satire to shine a light on what he considered injustices. But Jack the Ripper did in fact force Londoners and other Brits to pay attention to the breeding ground of crime and misery that Whitechapel was. The conditions weren't new, and some writers had tackled the issues before the crime spree. A writer named Margaret Harkness (who used the pseudonym John Law), for one, warned the well-to-do West End a few years earlier that "the whole of the East End is starving. . . . One fine day the people about here will go desperate, and they will walk westwards, cutting throats and hurling brickbats, until they are shot down by the military," she warned.

Whitechapel was a bomb ready to explode, and "the murders were almost bound to happen," as another writer put it in a letter to one of the newspapers.

Tensions Between the Police and the Neighborhood

Sir Charles Warren, the Metropolitan Police Commissioner who headed up the Ripper investigations, carried a lot of history—or baggage—into the case. Less than a year earlier, he was at the center of a clash between police and protesters when he issued a ban on demonstrations by thousands of destitute and unemployed Londoners at Trafalgar Square.

When the protesters made it clear that they intended to defy that order, Warren squared off with them to enforce the ban. An estimated twenty thousand demonstrators showed up for the action, and Warren responded with full force, deploying two thousand constables to form a ring around the square, two-deep, and another three thousand nearby in reserve. He didn't stop there, either. He also stationed a battalion of Grenadier Guard foot soldiers, and a regiment of mounted Life Guards at the ready.

Inevitably, perhaps, things got out of hand. By the time it was over, two protesters were dead and a hundred people were hospitalized. Forty protesters were in jail, and seventy-seven constables suffered injuries, according to the tally of one researcher. For his part, Warren emerged from the day—which came to be known as "Bloody Sunday"—as a hero to some and a villain to others.

The destitute demonstrators and their radical allies, of course, were in the camp that viewed him as a villain. That wasn't a concern for Warren at the time, when the voices of the Establishment were loud and unified in their praise for his actions.

But it came back to haunt him the following year, when he found himself heading up the ultimately fruitless police search for Jack the Ripper in the midst of the those same lower-class adversaries, who weren't inclined to forget.

The left-wing allies and press that condemned Warren in the wake of Bloody Sunday didn't forget either. For them, each police misstep, real or manufactured by the papers, was a chance to draw blood. George Bernard Shaw, who was a critical voice throughout the Whitechapel investigations, raised the specter of Bloody Sunday in one attack in which he condemned the "West End press" for "hounding on Sir Charles Warren to thrash and muzzle the scum who dared to complain that they were starving."

For Warren, the incessant bad press became a death by a thousand cuts, and just two months after taking over the investigation he tendered his resignation from his top post at Scotland Yard.

The Women of Whitechapel

During his tenure as Commissioner, Charles Warren also played a significant role in shaping the police response to prostitution and the lives of the women who worked the streets and brothels of London, including Jack the Ripper's victims.

By the time the killer began his spree, some sections of London—Whitechapel very much among them—were overrun by street walkers. It was difficult or impossible for a man to walk down certain streets without being solicited, according to numerous reports, and "respectable" women didn't even think of going out at night.

A number of factors combined to create that situation. The crushing poverty and chronic unemployment experienced by so many women was clearly one of them, and widespread alcoholism (a common trait among Jack the Ripper's victims) was undeniably another. But a series of policy decisions played a big part as well.

33

In 1885, an act of Parliament "to make further provision for the Protection of Women and Girls, the suppression of brothels, and other purposes" called for a tougher response to widespread prostitution, at the instigation of anti-crime activists like the National Vigilance Association. That group and others pushed for strict enforcement by police to "repress" the vice so "respectable" citizens didn't have to contend with it on city streets. (Interestingly, prostitution itself was not illegal, but solicitation was).

The effort to repress the activity, however, met resistance from police officials, including Commissioner Warren, who saw it as tying up resources and manpower that could be better used in other ways. Warren's opposition also had a philosophical aspect that was at least as important. He believed a crackdown in the areas where prostitution thrived would just serve to "[drive] them into respectable places." For that reason, he felt, it was better to leave the brothels and streetwalkers in their established places in the roughest parts of town and contain the activity there.

There were also legal and bureaucratic barriers that got in the way of cleaning up the streets. It was difficult to prove solicitation, so constables were reluctant to make an arrest that was likely to be dismissed by a magistrate. Arrests without ironclad evidence accomplished little beyond generating hassles and unnecessary paperwork for the arresting officer.

The upshot of it all was that by 1888 an untold number of women—solo entrepreneurs without pimps or protectors—were on the streets of Whitechapel each night. Desperate for money, and, for at least five of them, soaked in alcohol, they were eager to accept the advances of a probably unassuming looking man who turned out to be anything but harmless.

Part 2:
The Women He Killed

"I think she's breathing, but it is little if she is."—**Robert Paul**

Chapter 4:
Mary Ann Nichols

"I am settled in my new place, and going all right up to now."—**Mary Ann Nichols**

Mary Ann Nichols—also known as "Polly"—was the first.

And it was, in fact, a dark and stormy night, just like in the cliché.

The body was discovered at about 3:45 a.m., sprawled indelicately in a narrow street called Buck's Row. Her hands and face were cold, but her upper arms and legs were still warm to the touch, according to the two men who found her.

The men, both "carters" (drivers of horse-drawn carriages that were the nineteenth century equivalent of today's delivery vans), came across the site separately on their ways to their jobs. In the darkness of the rainy night, and with just a single gaslamp far down the street for what faint illumination they had, they weren't even sure she was dead.

"I think she's breathing, but it is little if she is," Robert Paul, the second man on the scene, said to Charles Cross, the first to arrive. Paul also thought he could detect a faint heartbeat.

Whether the woman was dead or alive, however, Cross and Paul had jobs to get to, and no time to get too deeply involved at the scene. They rearranged Nichols's clothing for the sake of modesty and went on their way, having decided to notify the first policeman they came across.

They did that when they soon met a Police Constable (PC, or what is also known as a "bobby") named Jonas Mizen. "She looks to me to be either dead or drunk," Cross told the constable. "But for my part I think she is dead."

PC Mizen hurried to the Buck's Row location. When he got there, he met up with two more PCs, John Neill and John Thain, who had found Polly Nichols as well.

And, thanks to a clear view from the lamps they carried and the professional opinion of a physician who lived nearby, they didn't have to wonder if the unfortunate woman was dead or not. By 4:00 a.m., Dr. Rees Ralph Llewellyn had completed a quick examination of Polly Nichols's body, and pronounced her dead.

As he was conducting the examination, the police, who were subjected to so much criticism as the crimes mounted, began a thorough and professional canvass of the vicinity, gathering a wealth of information but, of course, no answers.

The testimony Dr. Llewellyn gave at a later inquest showed that it was not a tough call. Her throat had been slashed, and one of the incisions, eight inches long, "completely severed all the tissues down to the vertebrae," nearly decapitating her.

But the brutality Dr. Llewellyn detailed didn't stop there. He also noted bruises on Polly's face and lower jaw that could have been the result of pressure from fingers and a thumb—possible signs of strangulation—and additional violent knife wounds.

He described several abdominal incisions, including a deep, jagged wound on the left side of the body, several incisions running across her abdomen, and "three or four similar cuts running downwards, on the right side, all of which had been caused by a knife which had been used violently and downwards."

The same knife was used for all of the cuts, he concluded, and he speculated that the attacker may have been left-handed, because the cuts ran from left to right. Llewellyn was also sure that Nichols had died "only some minutes" before she was found, and that she had been killed at that same place, although there was less blood at the scene—a "wine glass and a half," he calculated—than expected from the extensive cutting.

As the investigation progressed, police and doctors came to believe that the victims were strangled to death first, which accounted for the relatively limited volume of blood at the crime scenes. The bizarre "surgeries" that marked the Ripper's work were performed after the women's hearts had stopped pumping.

Polly's Path to Whitechapel's Dangerous Streets

At the time of her death, Mary Ann "Polly" Nichols's possessions included a comb, a white pocket handkerchief, and a broken piece of mirror, along with her clothing. That sad inventory didn't provide the police with any leads to follow, but it did open a window on the troubled life Polly had led.

She was born Mary Ann Walker on August 26, 1845 (her forty-third birthday came just days before her murder), the daughter of a sometime-blacksmith, Edward Walker, and Caroline. Her early life seems to have been unremarkable, typical of the working class at the time. When she was 18, she married William Nichols, and the couple had five children—three sons and two daughters—in what proved to be a long marriage, but one punctuated by numerous separations.

The final separation came in 1881, after about seventeen years of marriage, when Polly left home for good, leaving both husband and children behind. Whatever compelled her to leave—her alcoholism surely played a role, perhaps the major one—she spent the remaining seven years of her life moving from workhouse to workhouse, and from tavern to tavern.

At the inquest into her death, her own father told authorities that his daughter was "a dissolute character and drunkard," and that he had known that she "would come to a bad end." At the time, alcoholism was not treated as a disease, but more a personal failure of character, and she did not find much sympathy, as shown by her father's remarks.

In 1882, William Nichols discontinued the support payments he had been making to Polly when he learned that she was living as a prostitute, according to notes on the case. That prompted an effort by "parish authorities" to collect support for Polly, but William was able to argue successfully that she wasn't entitled to it because she was a "common prostitute." He saw her only sporadically after that, and not at all for the three years before her death.

Investigators assembled a detailed record of Polly's movements through the years, from the time she left the family home to her deathbed on the Buck's Row cobblestones. That path took her from Lambeth Workhouse, where she spent some nine months after losing her spousal support and to which she often returned, to a long string of similar facilities. (In nineteenth century England, a workhouse was a public institution in which the destitute received board and lodging in return for work).

For a couple of months in 1883, she returned to her father's home in one of many attempts she made over the years to put her life back on track. Sadly, her persistent drinking habits led to friction between them, and she left the morning after a major argument. She didn't speak to him again for four years.

Despite such conflicts, however, and the wear and tear of her life on the edge, people who knew Polly regularly described her as relatively low-key and "a very clean woman who always seemed to keep to herself." Even during his examination of her body, Dr. Llewellyn was moved to comment on the cleanliness of her thighs.

Polly's stints in workhouses were broken up when she lived for several years with a blacksmith named Thomas Dew. During this period, she may have found some normalcy in her life. By 1887, though, she was back in the workhouse and back on the streets. On December 2 of that year, constables found her sleeping outside in

Trafalgar Square, and sent her back to Lambeth Workhouse.

Polly Nichols made what was her final attempt to clean up her life when she took a job as a domestic servant, a position she was able to hold onto for two months. In July, she left unexpectedly and without notice, stealing three pounds, ten shillings worth of clothing from the lady of the house on her way.

Shortly before the theft, she had written her father for the first time since leaving his home in anger. Her letter brimmed with optimism, and particularly hope that she could finally turn a corner.

I just right [sic] to say you will be glad to know that I am settled in my new place, and going all right up to now. My people went out yesterday and have not returned, so I am left in charge. It is a grand place inside, with trees and gardens back and front. All has been newly done up. They are teetotalers and religious so I ought to get on. They are very nice people, and I have not too much to do. I hope you are all right and the boy has work. So good bye for the present.
from yours truly,
Polly

The Ripper Begins His Spree

On the night of August 30, Polly Nichols didn't have "doss money" (slang for the money needed to rent a room in a lodging house), but that didn't get her down. Tracing her last steps, investigators documented that she was seen walking down Whitechapel Road at 11:00 p.m., presumably soliciting. Thirty minutes after midnight, she was spotted again, leaving a nearby pub and headed for a lodging house.

Approximately an hour later, she was turned away from the lodging house, because she didn't have doss money for the night. She left in good spirits, vowing to get her doss money soon and come back. At 2:30 a.m., she ran into Emily Holland, a friend and sometime roommate, who later told police that Polly was "very drunk and staggered against the wall."

In a conversation that lasted for seven or eight minutes, Polly told Emily that, "I've had my doss money three times today and spent it." (The going rate for a prostitute of Polly's station was three pence, which was also the cost of a large glass of gin).

"It won't be long before I'm back," Polly said.

All was normal when PC John Thain passed down Buck's Row at 3:15 a.m. while walking his beat, and another officer named Sergeant Kerby reported the same thing about passing the spot at roughly the same time.

But it was far from normal when Charles Cross and Robert Paul, the two carters on their way to work, reached that same spot half an hour later.

Chapter 5:
Annie Chapman

"I must go out and get some money or I shall have no lodgings."—**Annie Chapman**

The bruises on her face and around her chin and jaw were new, although the two on her upper chest, each the size and shape of a man's thumb, and the one on her temple were probably several days old.

Her throat had been severed, deeply and viciously, the incisions starting on the left and wrapping around. It appeared to the doctor that the attacker had attempted to separate the bones in her neck.

Her face was swollen and her tongue protruding, both indicators of strangulation.

The wounds to her abdomen, which had been "entirely laid open," were extreme, too. The intestines were removed and placed upon the dead woman's shoulder. The uterus and the upper portion of her vagina, along with a portion of her bladder, had been removed, and were nowhere to be found at the crime scene.

He didn't have the name yet, but Jack the Ripper had struck again, only eight days after taking Polly Nichols's life. This time, it was 47-year-old Annie Chapman he targeted, and he had stepped up his barbarity even more.

Annie, who also was known as "Dark Annie" or sometimes as Annie Siffey (or Sievey, or Sivvey), was probably more or less sober when the Ripper struck, unlike his first known victim, but that is not to say that she was in better health. She was malnourished, pallid, and suffering from a disease of the lungs and brain that the examining doctor indicated could be tuberculosis or syphilis. The disease was thought to be terminal. On the other hand, she was not an alcoholic (despite having a "drinking problem"), was strongly built, and had "excellent teeth."

She was a latecomer to prostitution, only taking up the trade after the death of her estranged husband on Christmas Day in 1886, an event that caused her support payments (10 shillings a week) to come to an end. Whether she was an alcoholic, had a drinking problem, or was a "sober, steady going woman who seldom took any drink," as a friend said, remains one of many areas of dispute. But one way or another, her life was in a rapid downward spiral by 1887.

Annie Chapman's Life as a Married Woman

Annie was born Annie Eliza Smith in 1841, six months before her parents, George Smith and Ruth Chapman, were married. It is coincidental that Annie's mother's maiden name and Annie's eventual married name were the same, but at age 28 she married a coachman named John Chapman.

The marriage seemed to be conventional enough, and the couple had three children before separating "by mutual consent" in 1884 or 1885, perhaps due to Annie's disputed "drunken and immoral ways," as a police report has it. There was also a strong suspicion on the part of investigators who pieced together her life that John Chapman was a heavy drinker himself. When he died at a relatively young age, the causes of death were said to be cirrhosis of the liver and dropsy, an old-fashioned term for edema, an accumulation of fluid that can be caused by congestive heart failure.

Even though their marriage had failed, Anne was deeply saddened by John's death. It was one more loss in a life that also included the death from meningitis of one of their daughters and the institutionalization of their son, a "cripple." Annie's friend Amelia Palmer, a source of information for authorities about much of the dead woman's life, said Annie cried when she learned of John's death, and even near the end of her own life still spoke regretfully about her children, and that "since the death of her husband she seemed to have given away all together."

Annie Needs to Earn a Living

At the time of John's death, Annie was living with a sieve maker named John Sivvey, or a variation of that, in a common lodging house. Sivvey didn't stick around long when Annie's spousal support went away, and she found herself no longer able to piece together a living from the work she could do selling flowers and crocheting.

A sickly, poverty-stricken, middle-aged woman with no marketable skills didn't have very many options in the harsh London underbelly.

Annie was not as rootless as Polly had been. Certainly no one could mistake the last years of her life for a stable one, but even so she was more or less settled down in one place by May of 1888. Along with about three hundred other women and men with very limited resources, she was living—albeit one night at a time when doss money was available—at Crossingham's Lodging House, which was supervised by a "deputy" named Timothy Donovan.

She also was involved in a relationship with Edward Stanley, a "bricklayer's mate" who had given himself a fanciful second identity as a military pensioner and who sometimes paid for Annie's bed at Crossingham's. They were an unconventional couple, maybe unavoidably so given her profession and his fictional life. But they settled into a routine of spending Saturdays and Sundays together, until Stanley went away for most of August.

He returned on September 1, the day after Polly Nichols was murdered and a week before Annie met the same fate. There were wildly contradictory stories about the events that followed Stanley's return, but any version of them was enough to explain some of the bruises on Annie's body that soon became evidence in the investigation. Annie and a woman named Eliza Cooper, her rival for Edward Stanley's affection, got into a fistfight a few days later, at the lodging house or at a pub, depending on different versions of the story. In the same way, the cause of the battle was alternately a florin—a silver coin worth two shillings, one-tenth of a British pound—or a bar of soap.

The fight, wherever it took place and when and why, was of interest to police investigating Annie's death not long afterwards, because it explained some of the bruises on her lifeless body that the examining doctor identified as coming from previous injuries. Essentially, the information about Annie's bruising and black eye from that altercation allowed them to look past the unrelated wounds and focus on the actual killer's marks.

Too Ill to Work, But Out of Money

When Amelia Palmer saw her friend Annie Chapman in the early evening of Friday, September 7, Annie was torn between taking the night off because she was "too ill to do anything" and buckling down and going to work.

"It's no use my giving way," Chapman finally told Palmer. "I must pull myself together and go out and get some money or I shall have no lodgings."

At 11:30 p.m., she was back at the lodging house, asking permission to go into the kitchen, but still without money for a bed. Shortly after midnight, Frederick Stevens, another lodger there, joined her in the kitchen for conversation and beer. Annie was "already slightly the worse for drink," he told police later. Another fellow lodger, a printer named William Stevens, reported that he also saw Annie in the kitchen and she told him that she had gone to see her sister, and the family had given her five pence, although she had nothing left to show for it.

She left the lodging house at 1:00 a.m. and returned at 1:35, still unable to pay for her bed. After being confronted by the night watchman who tried to collect the fee, Annie went upstairs to talk to Timothy Donovan, telling him, "I haven't sufficient money for my bed, but don't let it... I'll soon be back."

The case file records that Donovan rebuked her then, saying, "You can find money for your beer and you can't find money for your bed."

It is still unclear where she may have spent the next few hours, although one highly suspect story a barman later told to a journalist was that a woman who matched the description had been in the Ten Bells pub at 5 a.m. He said she had a quick drink before "a man in a little skull cap" looked in the door and called to her to come out.

At 5:30 a.m., as confirmed by a nearby church bell, Elizabeth Long saw Annie with a man "hard against the shutters of 29 Hanbury Street," Annie facing Long and the man facing away. When she spoke with police later, she reported hearing the man ask "Will you?" and Annie answer "Yes."

At roughly the same time, or what must have been just minutes later, the man who lived next door at 27 Hanbury Street went into his backyard heading for his outhouse when he heard voices across the fence that separated his yard from the one behind 29 Hanbury Street. The voices were mostly mostly unintelligible, except for a woman saying "no," before he heard something strike the wooden fence.

Just before 6:00 a.m., John Davis, a cartman like the early risers who had discovered Polly Nichols's body the week before, found Annie Chapman dead in the backyard of the house in which he lived in a third floor apartment.

Chapter 6:
Elizabeth Stride

"...no one cares what becomes of us! Perhaps some of us will be killed next!"—**An Unnamed Prostitute**

Dr. Thomas Barnardo recognized Liz Stride as soon as he saw the body.

He had seen her just days before at the lodging house at 32 Flower and Dean Street. The doctor, who doubled as a street preacher dedicated to the improvement of the lives of London's most destitute people, had gone there to get feedback from the residents on a charitable idea he had. In the kitchen, he came across a gathering of women and girls discussing the Whitechapel murders, all of them "thoroughly frightened."

"We're all up to no good, no one cares what becomes of us!" he heard one woman he took to be drunk cry out bitterly. "Perhaps some of us will be killed next!"

That was on September 26. Liz Stride was found dead early in the morning on October 1.

A Killer Hiding in the Shadows

This time, the discovery was made by a jewelry salesman named Louis Diemschutz, who was driving his cart and pony into a spot called Dutfield's Yard at 1:00 in the morning. At the entrance to the pitch black yard, however, the pony shied and refused to go any further. Diemschutz couldn't see what was scaring the animal, but he used his whip to probe the area in front of the cart and found that a person was lying there, probably asleep or drunk or both, he thought.

Looking for help in dealing with the situation, Diemschutz went into the International Working Men's Educational Club located there and enlisted two other men, Isaac Kozebrodsky and Morris Eagle. When the three of them returned to the yard to investigate further, they realized they were not dealing with a hard-drinker who had passed out in the street.

They had found the still-warm body of Elizabeth Stride, also known on the street as Long Liz. Her throat was slashed in the familiar manner, but unlike the others, she hadn't been disemboweled. In all likelihood, Diemschutz had interrupted Jack the Ripper at work.

If so, it may not have been the first time that night that the killer had revealed himself. At least five possible sightings were reported to the police after the murder came to light.

Did Jack the Ripper Show His Face?

The first possible sighting occurred at 11:00 p.m., when J. Best and John Gardner entered the Bricklayer's Arms Public House. As they were going in, they told police, Elizabeth Stride was coming out, in the company of "a short man with a dark mustache and sandy eyelashes," dressed in a billycock hat, morning suit, and coat.

Instead of going out into the pouring rain right away, though, Liz and the man lingered in the doorway, hugging and kissing and attracting a lot of attention, Best said. "... and as he seemed a respectably dressed man, we were rather astonished at the way he was going on at the woman."

Forty-five minutes later, William Marshall, another laborer, saw Liz Stride standing in a doorway and "kissing and carrying on" with a man in a short black coat and a sailor's hat.

The next credible sighting was at 12:35, and it came from a bobby. PC William Smith saw Stride with a man on Berner Street, near the International Working Men's Educational Club. He pegged the man at 28 years old, and said he was wearing a dark coat and deerstalker hat, and was carrying a package.

The most detailed account came from a man who may have seen the murderer and his victim at about 12:45 at the same place Stride's body was discovered several minutes later. A file in the Home Office preserved his story:

Israel Schwartz of 22 Helen Street, Backchurch Lane, stated that at this hour turning into Berner Street from Commercial Road, and having gotten as far as the gateway where the murder was committed, he saw a man stop and speak to a woman, who was standing in the gateway. He tried to pull the woman into the street, but he turned her round and threw her down on the footway and the woman screamed three times, but not very loudly. On crossing to the opposite side of the street, he saw a second man lighting his pipe. The man who threw the woman down called out, apparently to the man on the opposite side of the road, 'Lipski,' and then Schwartz walked away, but finding that he was followed by the second man, he ran as far as the railway arch, but the man did not follow so far.

Schwartz cannot say whether the two men were together or known to each other. Upon being taken to the mortuary Schwartz identified the body as that of the woman he had seen.

It wasn't lost on the authorities that there were significant disparities among the multiple reports, including the two that were taken most seriously. PC Smith and Israel Schwartz both offered credible and detailed reports, but they differed in their descriptions of the man they saw. In the end, the sightings that night, like hundreds of leads over the course of the investigations, led nowhere.

Still, it was difficult to dismiss Schwartz's compelling story out of hand.

An Immigrant in London

Elizabeth Stride found her way to Whitechapel by a different route than the Ripper's other victims. For her, the path began in Sweden, where she was born Elisabeth Gustafsdotter in 1843, the daughter of Gustaf Ericsson, a farmer, and his wife, Beata Carlsdotter.

And, although she wasn't Mediterranean, Eastern European, or Jewish, she may have been very much the immigrant the proper people of London feared most. She left home at 16 to work as a maid. By the time she was 21, she was registered as a prostitute with the

Gothenburg, Sweden police, had been treated for venereal disease twice, and had given birth to a stillborn baby.

In 1866, she moved to London, where she may have worked as a domestic servant for a "foreign gentleman," according to one report, before marrying John Thomas Stride in 1869.

Stride, who was 16 years older than Liz, was a ship's carpenter and, from various reports, the marriage was often rocky. Nevertheless, the couple was at least modestly successful in business, operating a coffee shop from shortly after they married until 1875.

By 1877, however, they had separated, and Liz had been admitted to the Poplar Workhouse. The relationship may have been on again off again for a few years after that, but by 1881 it was over for good, and Liz was telling people that her husband was dead. In her bizarre tale, John Thomas Stride and two of their nine children drowned in the Thames in 1878.

In reality, they were childless, and Stride, who was still alive when Liz began telling the story, died of tuberculosis in 1884.

After the marriage ended, Liz became a regular not only in London workhouses and lodging houses, but at Thames Magistrates Court, too. She quickly racked up an impressive record of drunk and disorderly charges under an assumed name.

Occasionally, she turned to the Church of Sweden for alms, and for much of her last three years she lived in a volatile relationship with Michael Kidney, a dock worker. After her death, Kidney told the police that she had frequently left home for unpredictable lengths of time, but he never looked for her because she always returned, adding that "she likes me better than other men."

It may have been a fight with Michael that led Liz to check in to the lodging house on September 26, the day Dr. Bernardo saw her there, and just days before her murder, although Kidney denied that.

In any event, that common house was Elizabeth Stride's last address before she met the man she and the other women so feared—if she did in fact meet Jack the Ripper, that is. Some Ripperologists question that because, while her slaying resembled Jack's work in some ways, her body wasn't mutilated. Most, however, are convinced hers is properly included among the canonical murders, and that there's a simple explanation for difference in the M.O. in her case: Jack had been scared off, but he wasn't finished for the night.

Chapter 7:
Catherine Eddowes

"She was not often in drink and was a very jolly woman, often singing."—**Frederick Wilkinson**

When it comes to Catherine Eddowes (sometimes known as Kate Kelly), there are mysteries wrapped inside of mysteries. Like Jack the Ripper's other victims before her, she was middle-aged, destitute, out late and alone on the mean streets of London, and drunk or something close to that.

But there were differences, too. For one thing, those who knew her best told the police that she was never known to "walk the streets" soliciting trade as a prostitute. They denied, too, that she was a heavy drinker, although she spent the hours before her death in a police drunk tank after she was found collapsed in the street in an alcoholic stupor.

One man who was questioned by police about Eddowes's habits—Frederick Wilkinson, the deputy at Cooney's Lodging House, where Kate was well known for several years—said she "was not often in drink and was a very jolly woman, often singing." Wilkinson also said that he had never heard or seen anything that would lead him to think she was a prostitute, and that Eddowes was typically in the house for the night by 9 or 10 p.m.

John Kelly, the man Kate had been involved with since 1871, also denied that he had ever known Eddowes to engage in prostitution. She sometimes did drink to excess, he said, but that wasn't her typical habit, and several friends and family members concurred. Not everyone found her jolly, however. Others remembered her for a fiery temper.

She was probably the only Ripper victim ever described as scholarly and intelligent by those who knew her. She certainly was the only one who had ever made a living peddling cheap biographies along with her partner at the time, a pensioner from the military who wrote the books. During that time, one sideline for the two was publishing and selling "gallows ballads"—typically lurid confessions and accounts of crimes—to the crowds who turned out to witness public executions, according to a 1995 article in the Black County Bugle, which reconstructed Eddowes's life.

If that article can be believed (always a question when wading through Ripper-related media), Catherine Eddowes was not one to miss a business opportunity, either. When her own cousin was hanged in 1866, she was on the scene selling the gallows ballad she and her partner had prepared for the occasion.

Was Kate Looking for the Ripper?

There's yet another way in which Kate stands out among the victims: she may have gone out into the night for the express purpose of meeting up with Jack the Ripper. That, at least, was the story told to police by the superintendent at the lodging house in which she stayed on the night of September 28, although most researchers take it with a large grain of salt.

"I have come back to earn the reward offered for the apprehension of the Whitechapel murderer," the superintendent claimed she had told him. "I think I know him."

As the superintendent told it, he warned her to be careful that he didn't murder her, but that possibility didn't seem to concern her.

"Oh, no fear of that," he said she replied.

Nearly all Ripperologists dismiss the story out of hand, but some do take it or a related theory at least somewhat seriously. In the alternate version, Kate may have known Jack, but not realized he was the killer. If that was the case, she may have arranged an early morning rendezvous with him, oblivious to the danger she was inviting.

That might explain why she headed in the wrong direction—away from where she might find a bed for the night—when she was released from a cell in the Bishopsgate Police Station a little more than an hour before she died.

A Life on the Move

Catherine Eddowes was born on April 14, 1842 in Graisley Green, Wolverhampton, one of three children of George and Catherine Eddowes. She was educated at charity schools and by an aunt, and left home after she entered into a relationship with Thomas Conway when she was in her late teens or early twenties. (At the post mortem examination of her body, the coroner noted that the initials "T.C" were tattooed in blue ink on her left forearm).

It was when she and Conway were together that they traveled around the country producing and hawking their quirky books and ballads. Conway did the writing, and Kate focused on peddling the product.

There is no evidence that Kate and Thomas ever married, but they had three children and remained together until 1881. After they separated, Kate began a relationship with John Kelly, who "jobbed around the markets" for money, and who was her partner for the rest of her life.

In the late summer of 1888, Kelly and Eddowes left the city to go hops picking, as they did each year in the hops season as part of their pieced-together careers. But when they returned to London on September 28, they were essentially destitute. Kelly was able find enough work to scratch up enough money for Kelly to get a bed at Cooney's, and a bed for Eddowes at the casual ward in Shoe Lane, and they separated for the night.

The next morning, Eddowes, who had been thrown out of the casual ward for some unknown reason, returned to Cooney's Lodging House at 8:00 a.m. to meet up with Kelly again.

What little money they had was spent, and they spent the morning pawning a pair of Kelly's boots to buy food, which they ate together back in the kitchen at Cooney's. By afternoon, they were broke again, and Kate decided to go to her daughter's house to try and get some money. She and Kelly separated at 2 o'clock, with her promise to be back by 4:00. Unbeknownst to Kelly, her daughter had moved from the only address her mother had known.

That was the last time John Kelly ever saw her.

The Police Piece Together Her Final Hours

"I never knew if she went to her daughter's at all," Kelly testified at the inquest. "I only wish she had, for we had lived together for some time and never had a quarrel."

It was not hard at all for police to piece together Catherine Eddowes's last hours before she died; she spent most of them in jail. By 8:00 p.m., she was lying drunk on the pavement outside on Aldgate High Street, surrounded by a crowd and attracting the attention of constables, who took her to the station house to sleep it off in a cell.

By 1:00 a.m., she was deemed sober enough to go, after giving the police a false name.

That alias—Mary Ann Kelly—was seen afterwards as a tantalizing clue in a case already cluttered with too many leads and too few answers. Did it mean anything that the name was so close to that of the woman (Mary Jane Kelly) who became the Ripper's last victim more than a month later? Did the two women know each other? Did it maybe mean that Kate really knew Jack, and something of his plans? Where was she going when she left the jail, and why did it take thirty minutes for her to reach the spot where she was next seen, which was less than a ten minute walk away?

There remain questions about her death, too.

Her body was found in Mitre Square at 1:45 a.m. by PC Edward Watkins, ten minutes after a business traveler had seen Kate talking to a man he described as thirty years old, 5 foot 7 inches tall, with a fair complexion, a mustache, and a medium build.

As was becoming the familiar pattern, her throat had been slashed viciously, her genital area had been targeted, her abdomen opened and her organs cut or removed. But the killing also revealed Jack the Ripper's escalating fury in another way.

For the first time, he had also turned his knife on his victim's face.

"The face was very much mutilated," the examining doctor noted at the post mortem, going on to describe in gruesome detail dozens of wounds around her eyes, lips, cheeks, chin, and nose, which had been partially severed.

Police couldn't have known it then, but modern investigators recognized the pattern right away: with each murder, Jack the Ripper was growing more and more enraged.

Chapter 8:
Mary Jane Kelly

"All right, my dear. Come along. You will be comfortable."—
Jack the Ripper

It was 4 o'clock in the morning when Elizabeth Prater's pet kitten, Diddles, woke the woman by walking on her neck as she slept. And that meant Prater was awake moments later to hear someone cry out, "Oh, murder!"

The voice was faint, however, and a cry like that wasn't all that unusual in rough and tumble Whitechapel, so it didn't really alarm her, and she put it out of her mind. In a nearby house, Sarah Lewis also heard it, and also took it as just another outburst in the district.

About seven hours later, Thomas Bowyer knocked on the door of Prater's downstairs neighbor in McCarthy's Rents, their building. Bowyer had been sent by his boss, John McCarthy, to collect Mary Kelly's rent, which was six weeks overdue. The door was locked and no one answered the knock, so he moved a curtain back and looked into the room.

What he saw was Mary Jane Kelly's mutilated corpse.

Several hours later—after police had delayed entering the room to wait for a pair of bloodhounds that never came—a police official gave McCarthy the go-ahead to take an axe handle to the door.

The scene inside haunted the policemen for the rest of their lives, they said. Mary Jane Kelly's body was laid out on the bed, nude except for a chemise, her legs spread, her right arm nearly disconnected, her uterus, kidneys and one breast placed under her head, the other breast set down by her right foot, her face disfigured beyond recognition, her intestines placed by the right side of her body and her spleen by her left side, and all of the other signature wounds Jack the Ripper was known for.

There was a fire burning in the fireplace, Mary Jane's clothes were folded neatly on a chair, and her boots were set tidily on the hearth.

In a string of ghastly murders, it was Jack the Ripper's ghastliest.

A Life Lost to Mysteries

A lot is known about Mary Jane Kelly's death, but not as much about her life, at least not much that doesn't come from her partner at the time just before her death, a laborer named Joseph Barnett. And, for his part, much of what he had to tell was based on what he had heard from a woman known variously as Mary Jane Kelly, Marie Jeanette Kelly, Mary Ann Kelly, Ginger, Fair Emma, and perhaps others.

The story that has been provided largely through Barnett is that she was born in Limerick, Ireland, around 1863, one of eight or nine children in a "fairly well off" family. Her father, John Kelly, who worked in an iron works, moved the family to Wales at some point in her childhood, and Mary Jane was fluent in Welsh.

She was the youngest of Jack's victims, at about 25. By most accounts, she was the most attractive as well, a blonde, blue-eyed Irish woman "said to have been possessed of considerable personal attractions." It was not only her appearance that stood out, though, according to one of her landladies, who remembered her as "an excellent scholar and an artist of no mean degree."

Mary Jane was just 16 when she married a collier named Davies, who died in an explosion two or three years later, she told Barnett. Following Davies's death, she moved to Cardiff and began working as a prostitute, he said, although the Cardiff authorities had no records to confirm that.

She moved to London in 1884, perhaps working as a domestic servant, perhaps taken in by nuns, perhaps going to work in a high-end West End brothel. While she was at the brothel, she "frequently rode in a carriage and accompanied one gentleman to Paris," she told Barnett, but she returned to London because she didn't like the French capital.

A newspaper article told a very different version, but there's no reason to assume it is a more accurate one given the press of the day:

It would appear that on her arrival in London she made the acquaintance of a French woman residing in the neighborhood of Knightsbridge, who, she informed her friends, led her to pursue the degraded life which had now culminated in her untimely end. She made no secret of the fact that while she was with this woman she would drive about in a carriage and made several journeys to the French capital, and, in fact, led a life which is described as that 'of a lady.'

She seems not to have been in contact with her family while in London, although John McCarthy, her final landlord, said she did receive a letter from her mother in Ireland at one time. Barnett said she didn't correspond with family when he knew her. He and Mary Jane met in 1887 at a lodging house, and their friends considered them "a friendly and pleasant couple who give little trouble unless they are drunk."

A Big Strain on the Relationship

The relationship was apparently a good one overall despite financial strains, until late August, 1888, when Barnett lost his job and Mary Jane went back to prostitution over his objections. After Mary Jane's death, Barnett told officials and reporters that he left her because she was letting prostitutes stay in their room.

"She would never have gone wrong again and I shouldn't have left her if it had not been for the prostitutes stopping at the house," he told one reporter. "We lived comfortably until Marie allowed a prostitute named Julia to sleep in the same room; I objected, and as Mrs. Harvey afterwards came and stayed there, I left and took lodgings elsewhere."

Barnett may have left her, but he didn't go far. He remained close to her, and stayed in frequent contact right up to the evening before her death, when he stopped to see her at about 7:30.

After he left, Mary Jane went back into the streets, desperate for money for food and rent. Starting at 11:00 p.m. and continuing for about four hours, Mary Jane was reportedly seen, with and without a man, in several locations in the area.

But one of the reports stood out as both credible and potentially valuable in the effort to identify the elusive serial killer. A man named George Hutchinson told police he encountered Kelly, whom he apparently knew from the neighborhood, at a street corner near her home at 2:00 a.m. She asked him for money, but he wasn't able to help, having just spent all his money "going down to Romford," a large town in East London.

Hutchinson said they parted then, with Kelly commenting, "I must go and find some money."

A Witness Comes Forth

Mary Jane headed down the street, where she almost immediately met a man Hutchinson had passed just before running into Kelly. He saw her talking and laughing with the man, and overheard fragments of their conversation.

He heard Kelly say, "All right," and the man say, "You will be all right for what I have told you," Hutchinson later told police.

"All right, my dear. Come along. You will be comfortable," he heard the man say later, as they walked in the direction of Mary Jane's room.

The scene was illuminated by a streetlight, and Hutchinson, who stood on the street watching them talk and laugh and kiss, was able to provide a detailed description of the man's features and clothing.

He described a man who was 5' 6" or 5' 7" tall and about 35 or 36 years old, with dark hair and eyes, and "of Jewish appearance." As to that last trait, Hutchinson also said that the man had a pale complexion and a slight mustache, but that apparently didn't satisfy the press, who amplified the depth of the mustache significantly, almost until it was a caricature.

He was also able to provide a highly detailed accounting of the well-dressed man's clothing, and of the small package he carried in his left hand. The possible killer, Hutchinson said, wore a long dark coat, with a dark coat underneath it. His dark felt hat was "turned down in the middle," he wore button boots and gaiters (a kind of legging) with white buttons, his black tie was held in place with a horseshoe pin, and there was a thick gold chain around his neck.

"Respectable appearance, walked very sharp," the police report summed up.

The time and place and circumstances of that sighting make it entirely possible, if not probable, that George Hutchinson had just seen the first act of Jack the Ripper's final performance.

Part 3:
Who is Jack the Ripper?

"Kosminski was the suspect."—Chief Inspector Donald Swanson

Chapter 9:
Prime Suspects

"I would say it is a load of rubbish."—**An Unnamed Ripperologist**

For the criminal, the perfect murder is the one that goes unsolved. That's clear enough.

But could that same cold case also be the perfect crime for some of the sleuths on the other side of the chase?

It could if the unsolved crime is the most infamous one in anybody's memory, and there are still thousands of cold trails to follow in the hunt for any one of hundreds of potential and actual suspects. When it comes to Jack the Ripper, there's no end to either the horror or the fascination that still drive people from all backgrounds to delve into the subject and grapple with the clues countless others have already tried to crack.

Serious scholars and law enforcement experts have looked into the case since the day the killing began. So have journalists, historians, armchair detectives, novelists, conspiracy theorists, scientists, criminologists, FBI profilers, movie producers, tour guides, and who knows how many others.

Lifelong hobbies have come out of the study, and so have lifelong careers. For anyone who finds himself or herself among the millions of people who find crime and the criminal mind endlessly fascinating, it's the bottomless well of clues, theories, possibilities, and dead ends, that makes the Jack the Ripper case the "perfect" crime.

For some of those Ripperologists, amateurs and professionals alike, the case remains a baffling puzzle that is unlikely to ever be solved. Many others believe fervently that they have already solved the puzzle, pinning the killings on one or another of the people London police focused on at the time, but never charged, or on other likely—or wildly unlikely—suspects.

Well over one hundred men, and some women, have been named along the way, and there will doubtlessly be more persons of interest will emerge in years to come.

With so many unanswered questions surrounding the case, just about anyone who was in or near London in the late summer and early fall of 1888 can be a suspect—and many of them have been.

Was Jack the Ripper a doctor with surgical training? A butcher, meat cutter, or maybe someone who worked in a morgue? A woman trained in midwifery? A "moral crusader" striking a blow against evil? Someone striking out to bring public wrath down on the immigrant community?

Why did the crime spree start and stop so abruptly? Did the Ripper land in prison for a different crime, or in a mental asylum? Did he move away and continue his killing somewhere else, perhaps the U.S. or Australia, as some theories have it? Did he die? Did he just slip back into an unremarkable routine in a normal life?

Time has shown that there are nearly unlimited ways to fit the puzzle pieces together but, so far, none are definitive. For every insistent theory, there are detractors who argue against it just as insistently.

Still, after all these years, some suspects have come to the forefront, or stayed there from the start, and Ripperologists have settled on something like a consensus that they are the prime suspects.

Seweryn Antonowicz Kłosowski (George Chapman)

Seweryn Antonowicz Kłosowski was one of these prime suspects in the eyes of some of the investigators on the scene, especially Chief Inspector Frederick Abberline of the London Metropolitan Police. Abberline was considered one of the central figures in the investigation, in part because he knew the Whitechapel district intimately, having served there in various capacities for many years on his rise through the ranks.

Kłosowski was born in Poland in 1865, and emigrated to the United Kingdom sometime in 1887 or 1888, shortly before the Ripper arrived on the scene. He lived in Whitechapel and was working as a barber during the time that the canonical murders were committed, going by the name Ludwig Schloski. It was said, and memorialized in several books and the Pall Mall Gazette, that Kłosowski was Inspector Abberline's top suspect throughout the investigation. But, as with every suspect, officials could never make a case against him.

Time did prove, however, that Kłosowski (who changed his name to George Chapman five or six years after the murders) was a rotten apple, just as Abberline believed.

Eventually, he was convicted of killing each of his three wives, all of them with poison, and he was hanged in 1903.

The fact that he became a proven killer, however, did not end up strengthening the case that he was also Jack the Ripper—though he did pick up a different nickname: "the Borough Poisoner." Instead, it served to undermine the theory, because serial killers tend to pick an M.O. and stick with it, as critics of the Abberline's theory pointed out. More than a century later, though, Kłosowski/Chapman remains on the short list of suspects.

Aaron Kosminski

Another Polish immigrant, Aaron Kosminski (or Kozminski), was identified as a strong suspect by other top cops. Sir Melville Macnaghten named Kosminski as one of three leading suspects in an 1894 memorandum about the case. Chief Inspector Donald Swanson wrote a long-lost note referring to him in the margins of the memoirs of another important figure in the case, Assistant Commissioner Sir Robert Anderson. For his part, Anderson referred to Kosminski only obliquely in his book without naming him directly.

Macnaghten actually favored another of the three suspects for the killer, but didn't rule out Kosminski. Swanson, however, pointed the finger straight at Kosminski in the pencil notes he wrote in the margins of his copy of Anderson's book. The twist is that the notes didn't come to light until 1987, when one of Swanson's descendants made them public.

Anderson had written that an eyewitness had gotten a close look at the killer, and identified him "the moment he was confronted with him," but refused to testify. Swanson clarified this in his penciled annotation, writing "Kosminski was the suspect," and initialing it "DSS."

The witness refused to testify because both he and the suspect were Jews, Anderson, said, and he didn't want to be responsible for the execution that was sure to follow the killer's conviction. However, the suspect knew that he was found out and was being watched around the clock by the police, and stopped his killing spree.

Kosminski, born in 1865, was a Polish Jew who was admitted to a mental asylum in 1891, and remained there until his death in 1919. The theory that he was Jack the Ripper has both strong adherents and strong detractors, and so far attempts to test it using modern methods (including DNA analysis in 2014 that didn't produce conclusive results) have fallen short.

FBI profiler John Douglas weighed what is known of Kosminski's mental illness against what is now known about the psychology of serial murderers, and didn't find a match in that regard either.

Montague John Druitt

Of the suspects named in Sir Melville Macnaghten's memorandum, Macnaghten himself considered Montague John Druitt the leading contender, although he used faulty information, at least in part, to reach that conclusion.

Druitt, born in 1857, was a barrister—a lawyer—who was also employed as assistant schoolmaster, until he was summarily dismissed from the school post in late 1888, and committed suicide shortly thereafter. His death came shortly after the murder of Mary Jane Kelly, the last canonical victim, on November 9. His decomposing body was found floating in the Thames on December 31, 1888.

The timing of his suicide made him an attractive suspect for Macnaghten, who also claimed nearly twenty years after the murders to have "private information" from highly-placed sources. When he retired from police service in 1913, Macnaghten told reporters that he "knew the exact identity of Jack the Ripper," but wouldn't reveal it.

Those sources came to light publicly only a few years ago. It is now believed that a Tory politician named H.R. Farquharson, who lived near Druitt, and a close friend of Macnaghten's who was also connected to the Druitt family, each had shared their own suspicions with the police chief.

But there is no shortage of researchers ready to shoot down the theory, as is true of just about every theory in the case. For one thing, they say Macnaghten placed too much emphasis on Druitt's suicide in linking him to Jack the Ripper. Some Ripperologists argue that he may have been homosexual, a possible reason the school fired him and both a source of shame and a crime punishable by imprisonment at the time. They also note that there was a history of mental illness in Druitt's immediate family.

Others point to basic factual errors in Macnaghten's writings about Druitt, including identifying him as a doctor and overlooking a strong alibi for at least one of the murders.

Joseph Barnett

Mary Jane Kelly's partner Joseph Barnett did not rise to the top of anyone's suspect list until the 1970s, but he has become a serious candidate in the years since.

The theory, as advanced by a number of solid researchers, boils down to this: Barnett was deeply in love with Mary Jane Kelly, Jack the Ripper's final victim, and deeply disturbed that she had returned to prostitution when he lost his own job, shortly before the Ripper killings began. While the couple continued to see each other regularly, Barnett left the room they shared—the same one in which she was later killed—when Kelly allowed other prostitutes to stay there, and Kelly continued in her sex work.

Barnett was enraged by Mary Jane's decision, and likely by his own inability to support her. To scare her off the streets, he concocted a twisted plot to murder the other women. In the end, though, his plot failed, and he began to see that she did not feel as strongly about him as he did about her. On November 9, he took his revenge, attacking her with a level of fury that crime experts now know often indicates that killer and victim had an intimate relationship.

The argument goes well beyond that, too.

At thirty years old, 5-feet, seven-inches, and with a mustache, medium build, blue eyes, and a fair complexion, Barnett was a good fit for the witness descriptions police had to measure against. The theory explains the easy talk and laughter George Hutchinson observed between the two as they headed toward the house. Barnett as Mary Jane Kelly's killer also answered the question of how and why her body was found locked inside her room—the murderer had a key. Barnett, having lived there with Kelly until a short time before the attack, could come and go easily. Finally, if Barnett was Jack the Ripper, he would have no need to continue killing after Mary Jane's death, which explains why the murders ended with hers.

And, from the vantage point of the late twentieth century with the benefit of modern profiling, Barnett was an excellent match for the likely murderer described through an FBI analysis.

The FBI profile predicted the killer would have these traits:

- He was a white male, aged 28 to 36, living or working in the Whitechapel area.
- He had an absent or abusive father in childhood.
- The killer probably had a profession in which he could legally experience his destructive tendencies.
- Jack the Ripper probably ceased his killing because he was either arrested for some other crime, or felt himself close to being discovered as the killer.
- The killer probably had some sort of physical defect which was the source of a great deal of frustration or anger.
- And how did Joseph Barnett fit the criteria?

- Barnett was 30 years old, white, and lived within a mile of Whitechapel for his entire life.
- Joseph's father died when he was six.
- Barnett had worked as a fish porter, and was experienced in gutting and boning fish.
- Barnett was interviewed by police for four hours after the Kelly murder, and the police appeared satisfied with his testimony.
- Barnett may have had a speech impediment called echolalia (the involuntary repetition of someone else's words) according to news reports on his testimony at the inquest.

Of course, as in all things Ripper, there are people on all sides of the debate, but the theory seems to be a strong one, and it has gained traction over nearly four decades.

David Cohen

In the immigrant-heavy Whitechapel district, David Cohen emerged as another strong suspect who has been identified with "Leather Apron" by at least one leading Ripperologist. In the days after the first canonical Ripper murders, when shock and anger fueled anti-immigrant and anti-Semitic outrage, another man, John Pizer was taken into custody and held briefly as a prime suspect, as discussed earlier.

But in a 1987 book, Ripperologist Martin Fido proposed another Polish Jew as a suspect: David Cohen, as he was known to authorities, a violent and antisocial man who was committed to Colney Hatch Lunatic Asylum shortly after the murders stopped, and who died there the following year. At the asylum, he was considered to be violent and destructive. But he probably wasn't "David Cohen."

Fido noted that name was used in England at the time in the same way we use John Doe as a generic name today, although its usage was narrower because it applied specifically to a Jewish immigrant who was either unknown or whose name was too complicated. The author believed that the police on the Jack the Ripper case had confused the names Kosminski and Kaminsky, and that the confusion caused them to suspect the wrong man. The focus, Fido suggested, belonged on Aaron Kaminski, a bootmaker who had once been treated for syphilis, instead of on Kosminski.

Kaminsky had been living in Whitechapel, but after the middle of 1888, or shortly before the murders, his whereabouts were unknown. He could have disappeared during the Jack the Ripper rampage and landed in the asylum—as David Cohen—shortly after it ended. The idea has received support from John Douglas, the FBI profiler, who wrote in his 1989 book that the behavioral clues available pointed towards the man "known to the police as David Cohen... or someone very much like him."

Prince Albert Victor

Of all the people who have been suspected in the Ripper murders at one time or another, one of the most famous, persistent, and perplexing has to be the grandson of Queen Victoria, the son of King Edward VII and Princess Alexandra.

Prince Albert Victor, known to friends and family as Eddy, was born in 1864, and was widely regarded as beloved but backward, reliant on tutors at school, listless, partially deaf, perhaps mentally unstable, and with a low IQ.

But one thing he wasn't considered was a suspect in the Ripper's Whitechapel murders—not during his lifetime in any case. But—perhaps bizarrely, perhaps inevitably—he has been the centerpiece in any number of theories that have been built around the case. As with many others linked to the crimes, he only became a suspect many decades after his death, but some of the stories that have been put forth beginning in 1960s have all the palace intrigue of any Shakespearean tragedy.

Some of the most complex scenarios involve Freemasons, collusion with police, and various members of the royal family, including Queen Victoria herself.

In one version, the women were killed because they know that the Prince, who was second in line to the throne, was secretly married to—and had fathered a baby with—a Catholic commoner.

In another, Prince Eddy was exacting revenge after contracting a venereal disease from a prostitute, or that he had otherwise contracted a venereal disease that affected his brain and drove him to homicidal madness, an idea advanced in a 1970 book by a British physician, who also asserted that other Royals knew what was happening at the time.

Since the theory was first posited, it has appeared countless times and taken countless forms, from a book describing a palace plot to From Hell, a 2001 Johnny Depp movie that implicated Eddy.

Many experts have dismissed the idea that Eddy was connected to the killings in any way, either through using surrogates or taking matters into his own hands. They also insisted that there was no evidence that the prince ever had a venereal disease. But if anyone doubts the theory has staying power, they need only to look at newspaper articles from early 2016, when two letters from Eddy to his surgeon confirmed that he did, in fact, have gonorrhea.

That may lend some new credibility to one part of the story, but it did nothing to address even bigger issues, as one crime historian noted in the Guardian newspaper article announcing that the letters were being sold at auction. For one thing, Prince Albert Victor didn't come close to fitting the description police had. For another, he was known to be in Scotland at the time of one of the killings.

"I would say it is a load of rubbish," he told the reporter.

Chapter 10:
The Art of Murder

"I swear I struck not the first blow." —Francis Thompson

The mystery might have ended with the discovery of James Maybrick's diary in 1992, or with its publication the following year. Maybrick was a successful cotton merchant and a contemporary of Jack the Ripper, but he never emerged as a serious suspect until that book turned up a century later. Until then, if he was mentioned in connection with a murder, it was because his wife had killed him with arsenic.

But, like most things Ripper-related, the Victorian-era scrapbook that amounted to a detailed confession to the 1888 murders produced more questions than answers. For one thing, the diary didn't actually include Maybrick's name—it was signed "Jack the Ripper"— although it's true there was more than enough personal information in it to lead a reader to conclude that it was his. For another, Ripperologists were highly skeptical about its authenticity, pointing out contradictory and inaccurate passages, and most dismissed the whole thing as a hoax.

The diary, with the first twenty pages removed, was brought to light by Michael Barrett, an unemployed scrap metal dealer from Liverpool. Barrett provided at least a few differing accounts of its provenance over the next few years. In one version, a friend gave it to him in a pub. In another, it had been in his wife's family for many years.

Three years after the discovery, he swore in affidavits, twice, that he himself was "the author of the Manuscript written by my wife, Anne Barrett, at my dictation, which is known as The Jack the Ripper Diary." That wasn't the end of the discussion, however; he subsequently recanted that testimony.

Through it all, most Ripperologists maintained their doubts, and it's probably safe to say most still do. But several rounds of sophisticated scientific testing have muddied the issue. A number of scientists conducted tests on the ink to determine if the chemicals found in it were the ones found in Victorian-era inks, but different tests yielded different, contradictory results. Meanwhile, those who contend that the diary may be authentic insist that the testing proved its nineteenth century origins, and that only the police and the killer could have known some of the details it included.

Both camps have their adherents, of course, but the diary is also one important piece of yet another theory put forward by film director and screenwriter Bruce Robinson, who spent fifteen years researching the Ripper case for his 2015 book They All Love Jack. James Maybrick, Robinson concluded, was not Jack the Ripper after all. The real murderer was his brother, Michael Maybrick, a famous singer and songwriter.

Robinson's theory is intriguing in itself, but so is the fact that the popular musician isn't the only famed member of the artistic world to land on the list of suspects. Curiously, with Robinson's book, Michael Maybrick joins a roster of artists that also includes a noted poet, a famous painter, a popular actor, one of the creators of detective fiction, and, of course, the author of one of the most enduring children's books in the English-speaking world.

A Famous Singer-Songwriter Becomes a Suspect

Michael Maybrick, or as he was better known, "Stephen Adams," was a household name in his day. A noted musician, he was classically trained in piano, organ, and vocals—he achieved success both in Italy and England as a baritone—and by the 1870s, he was also a songwriter whose creations, first published under his pseudonym, "achieved extraordinary popularity." One, a sea song called "Nancy Lee," sold more than 100,000 copies of sheet music, making it a sort of Top 40 hit in its day. Other compositions ranged from romantic and sentimental to religious in their subjects and tone.

One of his sacred songs, "The Holy City," is still sung and recorded today. Another, the well-known "They All Love Jack," was an ominous reference to the famed killer in the eyes of some people.

He was often considered the equal of his contemporary songwriters Gilbert and Sullivan, and when he died one obituary writer had this to say:

When the news flashed along the wires that Michael Maybrick, or 'Stephen Adams' as he was better known to many, was no more, a painful sense of personal loss was created such as the death of few men could arouse. Who in the British Isles has not heard with irresistible appeal the attractive music of his many songs, all pure and enabling, some grand and devotionally inspiring in the sublimity of their religious feeling.

But he also was something more than a successful musician and composer, Robinson insisted in his heavily researched, extensively documented 800-page book. He was Jack the Ripper, and he could have been the poster boy for serial murderers, exhibiting a strong hatred of women, a "sociopathological" personality, and a massive ego, Robinson wrote.

He makes his case using mountains of documentary evidence, including letters and railroad timetables and much more, to place the traveling entertainer at the scenes of the canonical killings as well as at a number of other murder locations across the country, arguing that Jack the Ripper had many more victims than has been acknowledged.

Robinson also claimed that it wasn't the quality of police work in the case that allowed Maybrick to get away with his crimes; it was a conspiracy involving his fellow Freemasons, high ranking police and government officials among them, he claimed in an updated version of an old theory.

DNA Evidence at Last

Patricia Cornwell, the famous mystery author whose best-selling books are grounded in modern forensic science, settled on a different suspect, a painter instead of a musician.

To reach that conclusion, she applied current science to old documents that remain in the Ripper case files, and detailed the results in her 2002 book, which she confidently titled Portrait of a Killer: Jack the Ripper—Case Closed. Cornwell enlisted a team of forensic scientists to examine documents that might have linked to Jack (the famed "Dear Boss" letter and others) to detect mitochondrial DNA, which was then compared to mitochondrial DNA found on letters written by the acclaimed English painter, Walter Sickert.

Cornwell's team of forensic scientists found a sequence of mitochondrial DNA (mtDNA) on several Ripper letters that matched sequences found on several letters written by Sickert. Specific watermarks were also matched in both Sickert's letters and those sent to the police and media. If these findings are accurate, then, according to Cornwell, Walter Sickert was Jack the Ripper.

The German-born painter and printmaker had moved to England with his family as a child, and spent his early years studying art at some of Britain's leading academies before leaving school in his late teens to study with and work as an assistant to the famous painter, James Abbott McNeill Whistler. A few years later, he met Edgar Degas while visiting Paris, and fell under the influence of the Impressionist School. Ultimately, as a mature artist, Sickert gained considerable prominence as an advocate for avant-garde principles as a bridge between Impressionism and Modernism, and he was a strong influence on British art well into the twentieth century.

He was also known to have a great deal of interest in the Jack the Ripper case, and he believed that he had once stayed in a room that Jack had occupied as well, based on a tale the landlady there told. His paintings touched on a wide range of subject matter across his long career (he lived until 1942). Many were of theater and music hall scenes, interior scenes, nudes, and portraits (Winston Churchill for one). He was noted, too, for painting pictures in a series around a single subject. One well-known series was based on the "Camden Town Murder," the slaying of a prostitute who was killed in 1907, her throat slit in her bed.

For some, the paintings in the series are evidence that Sickert had an unsettling fascination with sexual violence, and he found his way onto the list of Ripper suspects before Cornwell ever took up the case.

Cornwell's was the third book in modern times to point a finger at Walter Sickert. A 1976 book tagged him as an accomplice in a conspiracy, again involving Freemasons and Royals, and a 1990 book concluded that he was the Ripper himself. Cornwell's evidence ranged from the DNA traces to watermarks found on letters to a theory—apparently unsubstantiated speculation—that Sickert had a "congenital anomaly of the penis" that left him impotent and fueled his rage toward women. Other accounts say he was a womanizer who fathered a number of illegitimate children.

The scientific evidence has been met with skepticism by many researchers. It may show a link between Sickert and some of the Ripper letters, but even that's open to debate. The DNA testing could only show that Sickert and someone who handled the letters shared certain genetic traits, but it could not prove those traits were associated with a single individual. Anywhere from one to ten percent of the population might have fit the bill, according to some scientists. Beyond that, however, most if not all of the Ripper letters were almost certainly hoaxes. Even if they could link Sickert to some of them with certainty, it might only show that he was one of the hoaxers.

Again, nothing definitive.

The Poet had a Motive

If it wasn't the musician or the painter, maybe it was the poet.

Not only did acclaimed English poet Francis Thompson write poems and stories about killing prostitutes both before and after Jack's killing spree, he had studied medicine for six years, during which he almost certainly gained a lot of experience dissecting corpses. He was also an opium addict who had lived a penniless life in Whitechapel before his discovery by the literary elite, and his only known romantic relationship had been with a prostitute there, who broke it off.

The end of the relationship, coupled with his drug addiction and other factors, drove him over the edge and turned him into a ghoulish killer, the speculation goes, and his darkest writing hints at a violent double life.

"I swear I struck not the first blow. Some violence seized my hand, and drove the poniard down. Whereat she cried; and I, frenzied, dreading detection, dreading, above all, her wakening, I struck again, and again she cried; and yet again, and yet again she cried," he wrote in an 1889 story that some see as a clue he planted in his work (a poniard was a small dagger).

It was Richard Patterson, an English teacher and author living in Australia, who turned the spotlight on Thompson in a 2015 book. Patterson had his epiphany in 1997 when he was still a student. He was struck by the convergence of the poet's sometimes grisly writing, his training as a medical student, his drug use, and his hard life on the streets of Whitechapel immediately before he rose to prominence. He was known, too, to carry a dissecting knife hidden under his coat when he walked in the rough neighborhood, and would have had his murder weapon always close at hand. Patterson's research was published in a short book in 1998 and an expanded work in 2015.

It was while Thompson was living with his prostitute lover that his talent was recognized and he gained the patrons who made him a success. But that otherwise fortunate incident had darker implications, too, Patterson believed. Because his lover thought he would be spurned by society and the literary world if they learned of his relationship with her, she ended it, causing him to have a mental breakdown.

Breakdown or not, Thompson went on to achieve great success as a poet, and continued to be admired by other generations of writers after his early death at age 47. Literary greats such as J.R.R. Tolkien, for one, said Thompson's work was an important influence on his own, and novelist Madeleine L'Engle used a line from his poem "The Mistress of Vision" as the title of her novel, Troubling a Star.

The Actor Who Portrayed Pure Evil

Then there was the actor, who didn't have to wait one hundred years for suspicion to fall on him. Even as Jack was terrorizing London, some people were looking fearfully at Richard Mansfield, an American actor who was appearing on the London stage in a production of Robert Lewis Stevenson's Dr. Jekyll and Mr. Hyde. His onstage transformation from good to evil was so convincing and unsettling that audiences began to think it might mirror reality.

He had opened the show shortly before the Ripper began killing, and by early October any suspicions that had already been whispered became concrete when the City of London Police received a letter that spoke openly about the fears the play provoked. Riddled with spelling and grammatical errors, the letter read, in part:

What I am going to Say Seems Allmost imposable but still Strange things have Happened at times. I have A great likeing for acters So that I should be the Last to think because A man take a dretfull Part he is therefore Bad but when I went to see Mr Mansfield Take the Part of Dr Jekel & Mr Hyde I felt at once that he was the Man Wanted & I have not been able to get this Feeling out of my Head....

The writer went on to point out that the murders were committed at nights when Mansfield was not performing (at the time, the first two of the Ripper's canonical victims had died, one just days before). The writer also said that newspapers had reported that similar crimes had occurred in America, where Mansfield generally lived and worked, and that the killer had never been caught. The letter was signed "One Who Prays for the murdrer to be Caught."

The rumors took a toll on the actor and at the box office. To try to win back public confidence, Mansfield offered to perform a play—this time a comedy—to benefit a social reform agency that was raising money to open a laundry to provide jobs for reformed prostitutes. That show was scuttled, however, when the bad publicity effectively drove him from the London stage at the time.

In fact, the bad publicity never really ended at all. When he died nearly twenty year later, his obituary in The New York Times remembered him as "the greatest actor of his hour, and one of the greatest of all times." But the praise appeared beneath a stack of headlines that read, "Richard Mansfield, One time Ripper suspect, Died 1907/ Created Jekyll & Hyde on stage at The Lyceum August 1888." Even today, his name is likely to show up on any short list of prominent suspects.

A Case for Sherlock Holmes?

Occasionally, Sir Arthur Conan Doyle is named as a suspect as well, although there's little reason to think very many people take the idea seriously. At the time of the murders, he was three years into his medical career and writing short stories on the side to supplement his income.

His accusers have generally focused on his medical training and his understanding of the criminal mind, as seen in the adventures of his character Sherlock Holmes, to link him to Jack the Ripper. Some also claim, without offering evidence, that during an 1887 stint as a ship's surgeon on a whaling boat, he had taken "sadistic pleasure" in the killing of the animals. That is about as far as the case against him has gone, however—and at least one recent writer has turned the tables to argue that he actually solved the crimes, not committed them.

In that scenario, Conan Doyle and Dr. Joseph Bell, his real life sleuthing mentor, were said to have known the identity of the killer. They kept it secret because they knew that Jack the Ripper was not Prince Albert Victor, as some believed, but his personal tutor, James K. Stephen. They decided to not go public with their discovery because it would bring disgrace to the Royal family, the story goes.

A Suspect in Wonderland

Sooner or later, every search for Jack the Ripper seems to find its way to yet another great artist of Victorian England. In this case, the suspect is Lewis Carroll, the children's author who created the fantasy worlds immortalized in Alice's Adventures in Wonderland and other books. He has only been even remotely suspected since author Richard Wallace tied not only Carroll (whose real name was Charles Dodgson) but also his colleague, Thomas Vere Bayne, to the murders in his 1996 book.

Carroll, Wallace said, essentially confessed to the crimes by placing clever anagrams—words or phrases made by rearranging the letters of another word or phrase—throughout Alice's Adventures in Wonderland and another book, both published the year after the Ripper's rampage. In addition to the word games, he claimed to have found numerical patterns in the texts, and speculated on possible connections among Carroll, Bayne, and Montague Druitt, a more conventional suspect discussed previously.

By scouring Carroll's writings and rearranging the text, Wallace came up with evidence like this, and in the opening sentences of his book declared the following:

This is my story of Jack the Ripper, the man behind Britain's worst unsolved murders. It is a story that points to the unlikeliest of suspects: a man who wrote children's stories. That man is Charles Dodgson, better known as Lewis Carroll, author of such beloved books as Alice in Wonderland.

Wallace's critics, on the other hand, pointed out that Carroll and Bayne had good alibis for some of the killings and no known links to any of them. They also noted that it is possible to mine just about any long text to find hidden codes, whether they are really there or not. To prove that, some have turned the tables on him and identified "secret anagrams" in Wallace's own work.

In that spirit, two anagram experts named Francis Heaney and Guy Jacobson turned the opening sentences of Wallace's book inside out, rearranging the words from the original passage quoted above to a tongue-in-cheek new version they posted on Ripperology and e-tail bookstore sites:

The truth is this: I, Richard Wallace, stabbed and killed a muted Nicole Brown in cold blood, severing her throat with my trusty shiv's strokes. I set up Orenthal James

Simpson, who is utterly innocent of this murder. P.S. I also wrote Shakespeare's sonnets, and a lot of Francis Bacon's works too.

But in some ways, there really may be a strong connection between Lewis Carroll and Jack the Ripper. Anyone searching in earnest for Jack the Ripper after all these years might find themselves traveling—just as Lewis Carroll's Alice did—down a rabbit hole or through a looking glass to a fantasy land where nothing is ever quite what it seems.

Epilogue

Jack the Ripper was not the first serial murderer. Undoubtedly, such people, twisted by nearly unfathomable forces and driven to destroy human lives for no comprehensible reason, have been with us forever.

One of the earliest accounts we have of the crime, in fact, comes from the ancient Roman historian, Livy. He wrote of a conspiracy among upper class Roman women in 331 B.C. that resulted in the poisoning deaths of an unknown number of men. At first, the deaths were believed to be from a plague, but a servant blew the whistle on the women. When the first two conspirators were arrested, they admitted to making a potion, but said it was for medicinal purposes and not for murder. They drank some of the elixir themselves to prove their point, and died immediately.

The Ripper was not the deadliest serial killer either, not by a long shot. A French nobleman in the 1430s was believed to have raped and killed more than one hundred and forty children before he was captured and hanged. In modern times, such murderers as John Wayne Gacy (33 victims), Jeffery Dahmer (17 victims), and the British physician Harold Fredrick Shipman (at least 250 victims) have been discovered and captured.

But it's safe to say that Jack the Ripper remains in a class by himself. No other killer has sparked so much interest, speculation, controversy, and intrigue for so long. Certainly, none has ever become a large industry in and of himself.

That may be explained in part by the timing of his arrival on the scene. In 1888, modern policing and detection methods were in their infancy, and newspapers on both sides of the Atlantic aggressively exploited and sensationalized crime stories to boost circulation.

No explanation, though, fully answers the question of Jack's enduring hold on the public's imagination. In some ways, that seems likely to remain an open mystery as well, just like his real identity.

Sources

Barrett, David. Who was Jack the Ripper? The suspects so far. The Telegraph 31 July 2015. Web. 3 June 2016.

Castillo, Juan. List 25. List 25 LLC, 7 Nov. 2013. Web. 6 June 2016.

Chan, Melissa. Jack the Ripper was renowned poet Francis Thompson: teacher claims. NY Daily News 6 Nov. 2015. Web. 2 June 2016.

Clark, Josh. Jack the Ripper Investigation, Hysteria and Press Coverage - How Jack the Ripper Worked. History.howstuffworks.com. Infospace LLC n.d. Web. 1 June 2016.

FBI — Jack the Ripper. www.vault.fbi.gov. Federal Bureau of Investigation 1988. Web. 10 May 2016.

5 People Who Were Suspected of Being Jack the Ripper. Mental Floss, Inc. n.d. Web. 16 May 2016.

Frater, Jamie. Top 10 Interesting Jack The Ripper Suspects. Listverse 8 Feb. 2009. Web. 25 May 2016.

Jack the Ripper Biography. www.famouspeople.com, 995 - 2006. Electric Foundry, LLC. Web. 13 May 2016.

Jack the Ripper in Recent Years. Biography.com, A&E Television Networks, LLC. Web. 10 May 2016.

Jack the Ripper source information. http://content.met.police.uk/Site/jacktheripper.

Metropolitan Police Service, London, U.K. Web. 13 May 2016

Jones, Paul. Who was Jack the Ripper? Not Aaron Kosminski says new evidence. Radiotimes.com 7 Nov. 2014. Web. 3 June 2016.

Jones, Richard. A Brief History of the Jack the Ripper Murders. www.jack-the-ripper.org n.d. Web 13 May - 10 June 2016.

Jones, Richard. Jack the Ripper History - Leather Apron. www.jack-the-ripper-walk.com n.d. Web. 25 May 2016.

Jones, Richard. www.jack-the-ripper-tour.com. Discovery Tours and Events, n.d. Web. 16 May 2016.

Laite, Julia. No 'solving' of the Jack the Ripper case will satisfy our obsession. The Guardian 9 Sept. 2014. Web. 23 May 2016.

Mallett, Dr. Xanthe. Is this the face of Jack the Ripper?. BBC News 31 August 2011. Web. 14 May 2016.

McLelland, Euan. Daily Mail.co.uk. Mailonline, 25 Feb., 2016. Web. 7 June 2016.

McLelland, Euan. Jack The Ripper suspect Prince Albert Victor is revealed to have had gonorrhea. Daily Mail Online 25 Feb. 2016. Web. 2 June 2016.

Nelson, Sara. Jack The Ripper: Poet Francis Thompson Named As A Suspect. The Huffington Post UK 11 May 2015, 5 Nov. 2015. Web. 3 June 2016.

Roberts, Marilyn. Albert Victor Duke of Clarence and Avondale and the supposed Jack the Ripper claims. www.englishmonarchs.co.uk n.d. Web. 2 June 2016.

Robinson, Bruce. They All Love Jack: Busting the Ripper. New York City, NY Harper 2015.

Ryder, Stephen P. www.casebook.org 1996-2016. Web. 10 May - 7 June 2016. Web. 12 May - 13 June 2016.

Scanlon, Gina. The 5 Craziest Jack the Ripper Theories. Ripper Street Blog. BBC America 14 Jan. 2014. Web. 3 June 2016.

Wallace, Richard. Jack the Ripper: Light-Hearted Friend. Melrose, MA: Gemini Press 1996.

Whitechapel Jack: The Legend of Jack the Ripper. whitechapel jack.com n.d. Web. 14 May - 3 June 2016.

Made in the USA
San Bernardino, CA
25 September 2016